Acknowledgement of Land & of the Traditional Owners of this Land

I would like to acknowledge the Gadigal pe
whose stolen land I stand on today.
I recognise that this land was never terra nu
these peoples was never ceded, given up, b
I would like to pay my respects to Aborigin
emerging, and I extend this acknowledgem
Strait Islander people.

*"I am DEATH,
the DESTROYER of worlds!"*

- *J. Robert Oppenheimer*

"The Don" UNLEASHED!
@ the "MoshPit", Newtown, 20.12 2023

CONTENTS

CONTENTS

CONTENTS

I Want to be Normal

(Voglio essere Normale)

I want to stop *hustling.*
I want to stop *hassling.*
I want to stop *struggling.*
I want to stop *fighting.*
I want to stop *stressing.*
I want to stop *pushing.*
I want to stop *forcing.*
I want to stop *scrounging.*
I want to stop *foraging.*
I want to stop *begging.*
I want to be normal.

I want to be like everyone else.
I just want to stop & rest.
I just want to be normal.

"Give me a home among the gum trees.
With lots of plum trees, a sheep or two, a kangaroo.
A clothesline out the back, verandah out the front
And an old rocking chair."

-"Home Among the Gum Trees"
-Written by: W. Johnson/B. Brown

"The Don"
30.07.2023

Complex Pleasures

(Piaceri Complessi)

I seek pleasures of the *flesh*.
I seek pleasures of the *body*.
I seek pleasures of the *HE♥RT*.
I seek pleasures of the *mind*.
I seek pleasures of the *soul*.
I seek pleasures of the *spirit*.
I seek pleasures of the *forbidden fruits*.
I seek pleasures of the *darkness*.
I seek pleasures of the *DIVINE*.
I seek pleasures of *Nature*.
I seek pleasures of the *Universe*.
I seek pleasures of *pain*.
I seek pleasures of *"tainted LO♥E"*.
I seek pleasures of *"unrequited LO♥E"*.
I seek pleasures of *"rejected LO♥E"*.
I seek pleasures of *"forbidden LO♥E"*.
I seek pleasures of *"tormented LO♥E"*.
I seek pleasures of *HATE*.
I seek *"Complex Pleasures"*.

"Tainted love (oh)
Tainted love (oh)
Tainted love (oh)
Tainted love (oh)

Don't touch me, please, I cannot stand the way you tease
I love you though you hurt me so
Now I'm gonna pack my things and go

Tainted love (oh)
Tainted love (oh)
Tainted love (oh)
Tainted love (oh)

Touch me, baby, tainted love
Touch me, baby, tainted love
Tainted love (oh)
Tainted love (oh)
Tainted love"

-*"Tainted Love"- Soft Cell*
-*Songwriter: Edward Cobb*

"The Don"
31.07.2023

My Sex Video

(Il Mio Sesso Video)

Early one Friday night, I went to a bar, trying to pick up.
I picked up an easy-going girl & asked her if she wanted to get high.
Her name was *"Dora the Explorer"*...
...and boy, was I in big trouble!

I picked her up...
...or more accurately.
...she picked me up from *"BED Bar"* in Glebe on a Saturday night.

We ended up at my *"Man Cave"* & as soon we walked in through the door,
she took off her clothes.
I was shocked!
I was like a little school boy with his fingers in the lolly jar.

As I was taking off my clothes, she saw my little cock!
She started to laugh!
"It's soooooooooooooooo small!", she screamed.
I said that it's NOT size that matters but how you use it!
"Size matters!" she screamed!
She then asked if she could use my phone.
My mind was too busy trying to get it up & then I got high.

As I was trying to put my little cock into her pussy, I saw my small cock
keep coming out.
As I bent her over from behind, she took my phone back.
I didn't know what she was doing.
But then, to my horror, I realised she was *"live streaming"* on my Facebook
profile!
She was posting a *"live"* sex video.

OMG!

I FREAKED out!

I grabbed the phone off her.
I deleted all the posts...
...but the damage had already been done!
It was seen by everyone...
...I even I got caught by my *"X"*!

I was really in the *"SHIT"* now!

My only defence, your honour...
...it wasn't me!
...I was framed!
...I am innocent!

But...
...everyone should make at least one *"sex tape"* in their lives...
...otherwise...
...they haven't LIVED!

Do you have a sex video?

"I'm a sex bomb.
I'm a sex bomb.
And baby I can turn you on."

"JLo" + "The Don"
03.08.2023

NOTHING TO DEFEND

(Niente da Difendere)

I don't need to *respond.*
I don't need to *explain.*
I don't need to *answer.*
I don't need to *protect.*
I don't need to *argue.*
I don't need to reply.
I don't need to *excuse myself.*
I don't need your *approval.*
I don't need your *validation.*
Because...
...I have nothing to defend.

I have *done nothing wrong.*
I have *acted properly.*
I have *treated you with respect.*
I have *acted with integrity.*
I have *been honest.*
I have *not lied.*
I have *not mistreated you.*
I have nothing to *be forgiven for.*
I have nothing to feel *guilty about.*
I have nothing to feel *ashamed over.*
I have nothing to feel *bad about.*
I have *no regrets.*
Because...
...I have nothing to defend.

My conscience is clear.
Because...
...I have nothing to defend.

"The Don"
06.08.2023

I Wanna Be Dumb

(Voglio essere Stupido)

I need to be *quiet.*
I need to be *silent.*
I need to *not talk.*
I need to *shut up.*
I need to be *stoopid.*
I need to be dumb.

Don't be a *"smart-arse".*
Don't be a *"smart alec".*
Don't be *smart.*
Don't be *intelligent.*
Don't be *knowledgeable.*
Don't be a *comedian.*
Don't be *funny.*
Don't be *dominant.*
Don't be *dominating.*
Don't be the *"centre of attention"*
Don't *take over.*
Be dumb.

"I wanna be dumb!
I have to be dumb!
How can I be dumb?
I wanna be dumb!
I wanna be dumb!
I have to be dumb!
I wanna be dumb!"

"The Don"
06.08.2023

Heartbreak Hostel

(Ostello del Crepacuore)

When your gal kicks you out.
And she tells you that she don't love you...
...in fact, that she never really loved you.
That she really actually...
...just played you...
...just used you.
...just toyed with you.
...just used you.
That it was just a game for her.
And you've got nowhere else to go.
There's a place where you can go...
...there's always room for one more broken-hearted sucker.
...like you.
And that place is called...
...Heartbreak Hostel.

So, if you downhearted & lonely.
All your friends have their own lives & don't wanna know about...
...your problems.
Or...
...travails.
And there's no one you can turn to...
...to tell your sad & sorry tales.
...of loss & heartbreak.
And you've got nowhere else to go
There's only one place I know of...
...there's only one place I can suggest to you.
Where its door is always open.
...24/7,
...365 days a year,
And that's...
...Heartbreak Hostel.

"Well, since I left my baby.
I haven't found a new place to stay.
I've been walking up & down Lonely Street
Until I reached Heartbreak Hostel.
Because I'm so lonely baby.
I'm so lonely.
I'm so lonely, I'm gonna die."

Songwriters: Elvis Presley/Mae Axton/Thomas Durden

"The Don"
06.08.2023

You Can Never Get What You Want

(Non Puoi Mai Ottenere Quello Che Vuoi)

You can *beg.*
You can *borrow.*
You can *steal.*
You can *hustle.*
You can *hassle.*
You can *connive.*
You can *manipulate.*
You can *lie.*
You can *litigate.*
You can *postulate.*
You can *argue.*
You can *fornicate.*
You can *pontificate.*
You can *theorise.*
You can *hypothesise.*
You can *try to buy.*
But...
...you can NEVER get what you want.
Well...
...you can try, try try.
But...
...you can NEVER get what you want.
So...
...don't even try.
Because...
...you can NEVER get what you want.

You can NEVER get what you want.
You can NEVER get what you want.
You can NEVER get what you want.
You can NEVER get what you want.

No, no, no.

You can NEVER get what you want.
You can NEVER get what you want.
You can NEVER get what you want.
You can NEVER get what you want.

"The Don"
07.08.2023

Oppenheimer Versus Heisenberg

(Oppenheimer Contro Heisenberg)

"I am DEATH, the DESTROYER of worlds!"
This what is claimed that Oppenheimer said after the first atomic bomb was dropped on the Japanese city of Hiroshima on 6th August, 1945.
Oppenheimer is the German nuclear physicist that defected to the USA along with Einstein, & headed the *"Manhattan Project"*, which developed the atomic bomb.
Einstein had developed the famous equation upon which the atomic bomb was based on.
An equation that has become the most famous & infamous in the world...
...E=mc2
...Emck
This equation changed the world FOREVER.
This equation meant that humans could now convert matter into energy...
...enormous amounts of energy,
...unimaginable amounts of energy,
...to harness the energy inside an atom itself.
...unimaginable.
...even "God-like".
...humans now had the power of a "God", in their hands.

But...
...what most people don't know is that Oppenheimer had a rival in Germany.
...who was also given the task of developing an atomic weapon.
...his name was "Werner Heisenberg".
...a colleague of Einstein but who did not defect to the USA with Einstein.
... it was a race to develop the atomic bomb first.
The different between Oppenheimer & Heisenberg was that...
...when asked how the atomic program was progressing...
...he apparently said that its atomic reaction was too unstable.
...and could not be controlled & was not ready for testing.
....Heisenberg lied to the German generals.
Oppenheimer, on the other hand, continued on and we all know the consequences...
...the first atomic bomb, called "Little Boy".
...was dropped on Hiroshima.
...the 2nd was dropped on Nagasaki.
...between 80,000 & 120,000 people were killed!

"The Don"
09.08.2023

People Are Strange

(Le Persone Sono Strane)

I tell you people are strange.
They do weird things.
Take a case in point...
...I was walking the other day in my old stomping ground of Five Dock shopping centre when...
...I saw my sister-in-law coming towards me in the opposite direction. She must not have been more than 20 metres away...
...I saw her...
...and she saw me.
I was just getting ready to say hi & tell her what I was up too.
When...
...to my complete & utter amazement,
...she made a right-hand turn,
...and ran into a shop.
I was stunned...
...even gobsmaked!
What the FUCK was that all about?
I couldn't believe it.
What did that mean?
I was shocked.
I kept walking straight past the shop...
...looking straight ahead.
I didn't look in her direction...
...just looking straight-a-head...
...walking at my normal pace,
...as though nothing had happened,
...as though the situation had not happened.
But...
...it did happen!

So...
...there you go.
People are strange...
...FUCKING strange!

"The Don"
10.08.2023

Humans Are a Bitter Disappointment!

(Gli Esseri Umani Sono Un'amara Delusione!)

Humans are a bitter disappoinment!
Oh yes, they are.
I expected more...
...much more!

Look at what they've done?
They've destroyed our *planet.*
They've destroyed our *Earth.*
They've destroyed our *home.*
They've destroyed our *humanity!*
I expected more...
...much more.

We had it all.
A beautiful *planet.*
A beautiful *Earth.*
A beautiful *home.*
A beautiful *humanity.*
And...
...we destroyed it ALL!

I expected more...
...much more.
What a bitter disappointment Humans are!

I expected more...
...much more.
What a bitter disappointment Humans are!

I expected more...
...much more.
What a bitter disappointment Humans are!

I expected more...
...much more.
What a bitter disappointment Humans are!

"The Don"
11.08.2023

I Know How to Be a Friend

(So Come Essere Un Amico)

I know how to be a friend.
Yes, I do.
I know what to *do.*
I know what to *feel.*
I know what to *say.*
I now all the requirements.
I now know.
I know...
...how to be a friend.

I can do it.
I can be a friend.
It's not that hard to *do.*
It's not that hard to be...
...a friend.
Just...
...a friend.

I know how to be a friend.
Yes, I do.

I know how to be a friend.

"The Don"
11.08.2023

(Condivido Il Tuo Dolore)

I feel your pain.
Yes, I do.
I REALY do!
That's what makes me human.

If I no longer feel your pain.
I am no longer human.
I have lost my humanity.
I have become an object.
I have become...
...a ROCK!

Don't *let this happen to you.*
Don't stop feeling *someone else's pain.*
Don't stop feeling *your humanity.*
Don't *become an object.*
Don't become...
...a ROCK!

I am NOT an object...
...I am NOT a ROCK!
Because...
I feel your pain.

"The Don"
11.08.2023

The Power of the Word

(Il Potere della Parola)

Words are so good!
They are like atoms.
Scattered in the Universe.
All I do...
...is rearrange them.
That's it!

I take words...
...from the Universe...
...and rearrange them.
It's that simple!

You can this poetry...
...I'll accept that.

But...
...remember...
...they just words...
...nothing more...
...nothing less.

But these words have power.
They affect the Universe.
This what I do.
I affect the Universe.
With the use of words.
Because...
...words have power.
And I use...
...the power of words.

"The Don"
12.08.2023

The God Particle

(La Particella "Dio")

The *"Higgs-Boson"* particle.
Two scientists...
...Higgs & Bosson.
Why is it called the *"God Particle"*...?
...and what does it do?
Well...
...this particle is the glue that holds energy together to form matter.
And so...
...since it creates matter...
...it was nick-named the "God Particle".
It was only theoretical until.
Because...
...the technology did not exist to prove its existence.
Until...
...the "LHC" was built.
"LHC", stands for the *"Large Hadron Collider"*
It is the largest *"Cyclotron"* ever built at *CERN* near Geneva.
It is underground, beneath 5 countries in Europe.
All co-operating together to build it.
It is basically a huge circular tube that has a circumference of 25 km.
Its purpose is to accelerate protons to the speed of light...
...in opposite directions...
...and then smash them into each other.
...and then observe what happens.
Theoretically...
...sub-atomic particles could be released.
So, called...
..."Exotic" particles.
Such as...
...the "God Particle".

Many *"doomsayers"* predicted that a...
*...huge *"Black Hole"* might be created & destroy the entire planet.*
Others suggested that...
... many smaller "Black Holes" might be created.
Also destroying the entire planet!

It was finally actually proven to exist when it was detected in 2012.

Humans had become God!

We had discovered *"God's"* secret.
We had discovered the ability to make *"matter"*.
We had discovered the *"God Particle"*.
We had discovered *"God"* itself.
And it's in ALL of us.
It's in EVERYTHING!
It is the basis of the Universe.

It is the *"God Particle"*!

And the world wasn't DESTROYED!

"The Don"
13.08.2023

Ascension of the "Virgin" Mary

(Ascensione della "Vergine" Maria)

August 15th is the day the *"Virgin"* Mary apparently ascended to Heaven.
A very religious day for many millions of people.
And also, a very contentious issue!
It's not as straightforward as it seems.
Or...
...should be.
The issue is not over whether she ascended or not.
No!
The issue is over how she ascended!
Did she ascend vertically or did she ascend horizontally!
This is the contentious & very controversial issue in religious theology!

It was so contentious & controversial that it caused a schism in the *"The Roman Catholic Church"*.
It caused a split...
...a breakaway.
Between the *"The Roman Catholic Church"*...
...who ascertained that the "Virgin Mary" ascended vertically.
And...
...the "Greek Orthodox Church" that resolutely believed that she ascended horizontally.

I, on the other hand still have an issue with the *"virgin"* idea!

"The Don"
15.08.2023

Don't Jump the Gun

(Non Saltare la Pistola)

Don't *rush.*
Don't *run.*
Don't *get too excited.*
Don't *fly before you can walk.*
Don't *lose your head.*
Don't jump the gun.
Because...
...you'll be caught with your pants down.

Take your time.
Follow the process.
Put one foot in front of the other.
Keep your wits about you.
Keep your head on your shoulders.
Keep your eyes firmly on the prize.
Whatever you do...
...don't jump the gun.

"Janie's got a gun
Janie's got a gun
Her whole world's come undone
From lookin' straight at the sun."

"Janie's got a gun
Janie's got a gun
Her dog day's just begun
Now everybody is on the run."

Songwriters: Steven Tyler/Tom Hamilton
Performed by: Aerosmith

"The Don"
15.08.2023

Passionfruit & Blood Red Oranges

(Frutto della Passione e Arance Rosse)

It started with prosecco.
I than added some passionfruit.
Then some mango & orange sparkling water.
And finally topped off with a slice of blood red orange.
That was only the beginning.
Something happened that I didn't expect.
When these ingredients came together a transformation took place.
Some might call it a reaction...
...a "chemical" reaction.
Something new was being formed.
Somehow the passionfruit & the blood red orange were merging into one
entity.
Something new was being created right in front of my eyes.
"Passion Red Blood orange fruit".
But then something amazing & incredible happened...
...it morphed into a fruit.
...a "Forbidden fruit".

The fruit of the *flesh.*
The fruit of *desire.*
The fruit of *passion.*
The fruit of *ecstasy.*
The fruit of *fire.*
The fruit of *sex.*
The fruit of *freedom*
The fruit of *Nirvana.*

Taste it.
Bite it
Eat it.
Swallow it.
ENJOY it.
Die in it!

"The Don"
17.08.2023

Just Like a Bullet Out of a Gun

(Proprio Come un Proiettile Uscito da Una Pistola)

A word...
...is just like...
...a bullet out of a gun.
A glance...
...is just like...
...a bullet out of a gun.
A look...
...is just like...
...a bullet out of a gun.
A stare...
...is just like...
...a bullet out of a gun.
A glare...
...is just like...
...a bullet out of a gun.
A frown...
...is just like...
...a bullet out of a gun.
A snarl...
...is just like...
...a bullet out of a gun.
A smile...
...is just like...
...a bullet out of a gun.

"The Don"
24.08.2023

You're a Disgusting Human

(Sei un essere Umano Disgustoso)

You're a disgusting human being.
You...
...burp very loudly & don't cover your mouth or excuse yourself.

You're a disgusting human being.
You...
...pick your nose in public.
...and eat it!

You're a disgusting human being.
You...
...fart loudly in public
....and blame it on the person next to you!

You're a disgusting human being.
You...
...shower only once a week.

You're a disgusting human being.
You…
...like Celine Dion.
...very loud!

You're a disgusting human being.
You...
...hate Bob Dylan.

You're a disgusting human being.
You...
...like musicals.
...in fact, you think that life is one BIG musical!

"Big G", "Troy" + "The Don"
26.08.2023

Words that Changed the Universe Forever

(Parole Che Hanno Hambiato L'universo per Sempre)

"I turn stone into flesh".

-Michelangelo Bounarroti

"I am Death destroyer of worlds!".

-Robert Oppenheimer

"We shall fight on the seas and oceans, we shall fight on the beaches, we shall fight on the landing grounds, we shall never surrender."

-Winston Churchill

"I have a dream".

-Martin Luther King

"Some men see things as they are and say why.
I dream things that never were and say why not."

-Robert Kennedy

"He saw wrong and tried to right it, saw suffering and tried to heal it, saw war and tried to stop it.".

-Edward Kennedy

"From little things big things grow".

-Paul Kelly

"I think therefore I am".

-Fyodor Dostoevsky

"God is DEAD!".

-Friedrich Nietzsche

"One small step for man, one giant leap for mankind."

-Neil Armstrong

"I am woman hear me roar!"

-Helen Reddy

"He ain't heavy, he's my brother."

-The Hollies

"Matter (atom) is just mostly empty space".

-Ernest Rutherford

"Sisters can do it for themsleves".

-Annie Lennox

"The Don"
28.08.2023

JUST TAKE WHAT YOU NEED

(Prendi Semplicemente Quello Che Ti Serve)

We all transform things.
That is a sign of being Human.
This is what differentiates us from all other living things.
We transform Nature.
Always have done so.
Since the moment we began to walk...
...maybe even earlier.

Even First Nations People transformed Nature.
They manipulated land.
You could even say, they *"manicured"* it
.

The only difference between them & us, today...
...is they did it with "Balance".
They took just what they *"needed"*.
They did not take MORE than they needed.

We do not have any *"Balance"*.
We do not take just what we need.
We take more than what we *"need"*.
Much more!

Do not take more than you *"need"*.
Just take what you "need".

"Take what you need & leave the rest...
...but you should NEVER take the very best!"

-Written by: Robbie Robertson
Performed by: The Band

"The Don"
28.08.2023

Who Knows Which Way the Wind Blows?

(Chissà da Che Parte Soffia il Vento?)

Do I have the wind behind my back?
Do have wind in my sails?
Is it just a light zephyr?
Or is it blowing a hurricane?
I think it's dead calm.
Because…
…I don't know which way the wind blows.

Is it blowing straight at me?
Pushing me back to where I started from.
Am I just "pissing in the wind"?
I can taste the salt on my lips...
...and it tastes good!
I fighting a losing battle.
Because…
…I don't know which way the wind blows.

It's tough out here.
There's a gale a-brewing.
Am I ready for it?
Do I have the strength to confront it?
Do I have the mental will power?
Do I have the spiritual integrity?
Can I survive?
Because…
…I don't know which way the wind blows.

It's constantly changing directions.
It's playing with me.
It's taunting me.
It's messing with my head.
I think it's got the better of me.
I can't get a handle on it.
It's a tricky wind.
I have to keep my wits about me.
Can I keep it up?

It is relentless.
It doesn't give up.
I'm getting tired.
I'm getting fatigued.
It's got me by the balls...
...and it won't let go!
I look up to the sky...
...but it is not going to help me.
I think it's on the wind's side.
Because…
...I don't know which way the wind blows.

I've gotta be ready for anything!
Because…
...I don't know which way the wind blows.

Am I up for it?

Maybe!
Maybe not!
Because…
...I don't know which way the wind blows.

"The Don"
02.09.2024

In Your Eyes

(Nei tuoi Occhi)

Do have the *light?*
Do you have the *fire?*
Do you have the *wisdom?*
Do you have the *freedom?*
I can tell if you do.
Because...
...I can see it in your eyes.

Do you have *"bright"* eyes?
Do you have *clarity in your eyes?*
Do you have *warmth in your eyes?*
Do you have *intelligence in your eyes?*
Do you have *kindness in your eyes?*
Do you have *LO❤E in your eyes?*
I can tell if you do.
Because...
...I can see it in your eyes.

Or...
...do you have...
...blackness in your eyes?
...sullen & bleak?
...full of misery & despair?
...fear & loathing?

Is there...
...hatred in your eyes?
...anger in your eyes?
...revenge in your eyes?
...DEATH in your eyes?
I can tell if you do.
Because...
...I can see it in your eyes.

"The Don"
03.09.2023

SAY NOTHING

(Dire Niente)

If you are...
...questioned.

Say nothing.

If you are...
...accused.

Say nothing.

If you are...
...blamed.

Say nothing.

If you are...
...asked why.

Say nothing.

If you are...
...doubted.

Say nothing.

If you are...
...asked to explain.

Say nothing.

If you are...
...put down.

Say nothing.

If you are...
...asked to defend yourself.

Say nothing.

If you are...
...asked to explain your actions.

Say nothing.

If you are...
...overlooked.

Say nothing.

If you are...
...rejected.

Say nothing.

If you are...
...abandoned.

Say nothing.

Because...
...you don't have to say a thing!
You don't have to justify yourself to anyone.

So...
...just,
Say nothing!

It speaks very LOUDLY!

"The Don"
04.09.2023

Walk Away

(Andarsene)

Turn around.
Walk away.
Don't turn around.
Don't look back.
Don't run.
Walk straight ahead.
Hold your head held high.
Walk proud & tall.
Just keep on walkin'.
Let your feet do the talkin'.
And keep on walkin'.
Never look back!
Never go back!
Just...
...walk away.

"These boots were made for walkin'
And that's just what they will do.
One of these days...
...these boots are gonna all over you!

Are you ready boots?
Start a-walkin'!"

"These Boots are Made for Walkin'!"
-Nancy Sinatra

"The Don"
04.09.2023

Less is More, More is Less

(Meno è di Più, Più è di Meno)

It's a conundrum.
How is this possible?
Is it even true?
It seems counter-intuitive...
...contradictory.
...illogical even.
That...
...less is more & more is less!

It's a question of balance.
Too much & you tip the balance.
Too less keeps you wanting more.

The question is to find the line between less & more.
The pivotal point which tips the scale.
Where less becomes more.

It's all about *intuition*.
It's all about *equilibrium*.
It's all about *balance*.

But one thing is certain...
...less is more & more is less.

"The Don"
04.09.2023

I Don't Let Anything Bring Me Down

(Non Lascio Che Nulla Mi Abbatta)

You can't bring me down.
Bad words can't bring me down.
"Drama Queens" can't bring me down.
Ignorance can't bring me down.
Stoopidity can't bring me down.
Ignorance can't bring me down.
"Fuckwits" can't bring me down.
Discrimination can't bring me down.
Racists can't bring me down.
Arseholes can't bring me down.
Greed can't bring me down.
Jealousy can't bring me down.
Revenge can't bring me down.
Hatred can't bring me down.
Cruelty can't bring me down.
A "Broken HE❤RT" can't bring me down.
LO❤E can't bring me down.
Society can't bring me down.
The World can't bring me down.
Politicians can't bring me down.
Capitalism can't bring me down.
Wars can't bring me down.
I can't bring me down.
You can't bring me down.
No one can bring me down.
I won't allow anything bring me down.
I won't allow anyone bring me down.

"You got me runnin', goin' out of my mind
You got me thinkin' that I'm wastin' my time

Don't bring me down
No, no, no, no, no
Ooh-ooh-hoo
I'll tell you once more before I get off the floor
Don't bring me down."

-*"Don't Bring Me Down"-ELO*
-*Songwriter: Jeff Lynne*

"The Don"
06.09.2023

The Monkey Girl & The Pussycat

(La Ragazza Scimmia e la Gattina)

She's a *monkey*.
She's a *"Monkey Girl"*.
She's *feral*.
She's *wild*.
She's *CRAAAAAAZZZZZZZZYYYY*!
She *eats with her hands*.
She *never washes*.
She *smells of "Nature"*
She's *untamed*!
She'll *tell you to "FUCK OFF"*!
She's a *"Monkey Girl"*!

She's *a pussycat*.
She's *soft*.
She's *cuddly*.
She *purrs*.
She likes to be *held*.
She likes to be *hugged*.
She loves to be *kissed...*
...all over.
She's as *"cute as a button"*!
She *LO*❤*ES to make LO*❤*E.*
She's *a pussycat!*

"The Don"
08.09.2023

Try Before You Commit

(Prova Prima di Impegnarti)

Sample the goods first.
Check them out.
Take them for a ride.
Take them for *"test-drive"*.
Check what's in the package.
Make sure that everything is there.
That there are no missing parts or items.
(You don't want to go hassling afterwards to get a refund or a replacement part).
Make sure they're not a *"lemon"*.
(Remember, 33% of all goods manufactured are defective!)
Don't commit with your eyes closed.
Do your research first.
Get informed.
Be informed.
Ask questions.
Check out the documentation.
Read the *"fine"* print.
Make sure there are no hidden clauses.
Confirm that they have a *"returns"* policy.
Ask about their warranty policy.
But most importantly...
...try before you buy!
Then...
...and ONLY then.
Commit!

"The Don"
09.09.2023

What Doesn't Kill You

(Ciò Che Non Ti Uccide)

What doesn't kill you...
...makes you stronger!
That's what you've gotta remember.

"The Don"
09.09.2023

Democracy is a BITCH!

(La Democrazia è Una PUTTANA!)

Sometimes...
...Democracy is a BITCH!

"The Don"
13.09.2023

THE PAST IS ALWAYS CLOSE BEHIND

(Il Passato è Sempre lì Dietro)

The Past is tied to you.
The Past is tied to your back.
You carry it like a cross.
It weighs you down.
You feel tired.
You wanna give up.
You start asking questions.
Such as...
...*"Can I get rid of this FUCKING weight off my FUCKING back!"*
...*"Is this FUCKING journey even worth it?"*
...*"FUCK this shit!"*
...*"I'm gonna QUITE!"*

But it's STILL there.
The Past is ALWAYS there!
Because...
...*the Past is ALWAYS close behind!*

"The Don"
13.09.2023

The "Big Bang" Theory

(La Teoria del "Big Bang")

The *"Big Bang"* Theory is NO theory.
It's a fact!
We were conceived with a *"big bang"*...
...and lots of grunts & groans!

"The Don"
17.09.2023

You Can't Change Someone Else's Mind

(Non Puoi Cambiare la Mente di Qualcun Altro)

You can't change someone else's mind.
That's our BIGGEST mistake.
Because...
...we THINK that we CAN!

"The Don"
18.09.2023

Power & Greed

(Potere e Avidità)

"Power & greed...
...and corruptible seed.
Is ALL there is!"

"No One Can Sing the Blues like, 'Blind' Willie McTell"

-Bob Dylan

"The Don"
18.09.2023

I Am A TOTALLY New Person

(Sono Una Persona TOTALMENTE Nuovo)

I have *shed my skin.*
I have *dropped my cross.*
I have *shaken off my load.*
I have *torn off my skin.*
I have *been reborn.*
I have *"shuffled off my moral skin".*
I am a Totally new person.

"The Don"
19.09.2023

The World Won't Stand Still

(Il Mondo Non Si Fermerà)

No matter what I *say*.
No matter what I *do*.
No matter what I *think*.
No matter what I *feel*.
The World won't stand still.

I can *jump up & down*.
I can *scream & shout*.
I can *let it all hang out*.
I can pray to *God*.
I can pray to *Allah*.
I can pay to the *Devil*.
I can pray to the *Universe*.
But…
…the World won't stand still.

That's the way of the Cosmos.
There's nothing you can do about it.
You just have to accept is fact...
...the World won't stand still.

And there's NOTHING you can do about it!

"The Don"
21.09.2024

How Old Are you?

(Quanti Anni Hai?)

How old are you?
As old as the *Earth*.
As old as the *stars*.
As old as the *Universe*.

How old are you?

Quanti anni hai?
Vecchio quanto *la Terra*.
Vecchio quanto *le stelle*.
Vecchio quanto *l'Universo*.

Quanti anni hai tu?

"The Don"
23.09.2023

What Do You Have to Say?

(Che Cosa Hai da Dire?)

What do you have to say?
NOTHING...
...and EVERYTHING!

"The Don"
23.09.2023

One Being Born, One Dying

(Uno Nasce, Uno Muore)

Imagine...
...if you will.
A moment in time.
As one person is being born...
...another is dying.

Imagine now...
...if by chance...
...they were to meet...
...travelling in the opposite directions.
Would they say anything to each other...?
...in that split moment?
What would they say to each other?

I imagine that one dying would say...
..."Have a good life!"

I imagine the one being born would say...
..."Have a good Death!"

"The Don"
23.09.2023

I'm Not Scared of the Darkness

(Non Ho Paura dell'Oscurità)

I'm not scared of the darkness...
...not anymore!
I used to be scared.
When I was a child of about 6 years old...
...I was TERRIFIED of the darkness!
I used to put my head under the blankets & wonder if this was what Death
would be like.
Complete *DARKNESS!*
Enveloped by the *DARKNESS.*
Engulfed by the *DARKNESS.*
Consumed by the *DARKNESS.*
Subsumed by the *DARKNESS.*
Submerged in the *DARKNESS.*
I was scared!
PETRIFIED, in fact!
The DARKNESS was out to get me.
The DARKNESS was my enemy!

But now that I'm so much older...
...I accept the DARKNESS.
I let it swallow me.
I breathe in the DARKNESS.
I give in to it.
I accept it.
I accept the DARKNESS.
I am not afraid of the DARKNESS!
Not anymore!
The DARKNESS is no longer trying to get me.
The DARKNESS is now my friend!

"The Don"
25.09.2023

The End

(Fine)

"The End" is not really the end...
...it's actually a new beginning.
...a new adventure.
...a new path.
...a new portal.
...a new future.
With...
...new opportunities.
...new chances.
...new risks.
...new hazards.
...new dangers.
...new rewards.
And yes...
...there will be rewards aplenty.
But most importantly...
...there will be closure!
"The End" shuts the door to the past.
So...
...don't be sad.
Celebrate...
... "The End".

"This is the end,
My friend, the end.
My only friend, the end."

-Written by: Jim Morrison
-Performed by: The Doors

"The Don"
29.09.2023

I'm Just a Poet in this CRAZY World

(Sono Solo Un Poeta in Questo Mondo PAZZO)

I'm just a poet in this Crazy world.
Trying to make sense of all the nonsense.
Trying to make my way through life without causing too much damage
along the way.
Questioning everything around me.
Outside of me...
...and inside of me.
My...
...thoughts,
...feelings,
...ideas,
...attitudes,
...beliefs,
...behaviour,
...actions.
My very existence.
Even *"Reality"* itself.

So...
...don't shoot me!
I'm just a poet in this CRAZY world.

"The Don"
29.09.2023

I'M COMPLICATED

(Sono complicato)

"I'm complicated!"
That's what she said.
I started to think...
...*"What the FUCK does that mean?"*
"I'm complicated!"
That means absolutely NOTHING!
"Get FUCKED!"
I'm FUCKING complicated!
Tell me something new!
I'm complicated!
"Who FUCKING gives a SHIT!"
FUCK OFF!

"I'm COMPLICATED!"
"I'm COMPLICATED!"
"I'm COMPLICATED!"
"I'm COMPLICATED!"

"Oh YEAH!"
"Get FUCKED!"
"Complicated my ARSE!"

"The Don"
02.10.2023

Ketamine

(Ketamina)

I was at a party.
She came over & sat next to me.
"Would you like some of this?"
I looked at her...
...she was holding a small vile containing a yellow liquid.
"What is it?"
I asked.
"Ketamine".
She replied.
"Catnip?"
I replied.
She started to laugh...
..."No! Ketamine!"
"It's sometimes called "Special K"".
"What's that?"
I asked.
"It's "horse tranquiliser"".
"Horse tranquiliser! WTF!"
"Yeah, it's used to tranquilise horses."
"I figured!", I said.
"It's ok to take it, in small doses".
"It makes you "trip". A bit like taking ACID."
"You put some & sniff it up one nostril".
"Like this".
Showing me how to do it.
"Wanna try it?"
"Sure!"
I said.

"The Don"
02.10.2023

Eva, Eve

(Eva, Eve)

Eva, Eva...
...the first woman.
Who was she?
Where did she come from?
Did she even EXIST?

Was she...
...beautiful?
...alluring?
...seductive?
...manipulative?
...conniving?
...deceitful?
...revengeful?
...strong?
...motherly?
...caring?
...loving?

The answer is there for all to see...
...right under our noses...
...staring us in the face.

Eva (Eve) is in ALL woman!

"The Don"
10.10.2023

The Sea of Death

(Il Mare della Morte)

We are born on the mountain top.
This is the happiest moment of our lives.
It's then ALL downhill from there.
Down the *"Savage River"*.
Until we reach the sea.
It's not the *"Sea of Tranquillity"*.
Nor is it the *"Sea of Peace"*.
Neither is it the *"Sea of LO❤E"*.
It ain't the *"Sea of Fortune"*.
It is...
...the "Sea of Death".
No one gets out alive.
Once you reach the *"Sea of Death"*...
...you will DIE!
You cannot escape

There are many stories of spirits that have arisen from its murky depths.
Songs have been written & sung.
Some have even claimed to have seen some walk on the water.
I don't believe any of this.
I have swum in the *"Sea of Death"* once & I was saved.
I was lucky that time.
I won't be as lucky next time.
The next time I swim in the *"Sea of Death"*.

"The Don"
11.10.2023

The Oppressed Will ALWAYS Win

(Gli Oppressi Vinceranno SEMPRE)

History has repeatedly shown over & over again...
...that the oppressors cannot maintain their oppression forever.
It requires too much energy...
...too much time.
...too much money.
...too much ignorance.
...too much cruelty.
...too much hatred.
...too many lies.
And...
...eventually
...over time
Their power will diminish.
And...
...they will be DEFEATED!
The question is of time...
...how long will this take?
Maybe it won't happen in one *"lifetime"*!
Maybe it will take *"millennia"*!
But one thing is for certain...
...it is engraved in stone.
...the OPPRESSED will ALWAYS win!

"The Don"
15.10.2023

Sexually Active

(Sessualmente Attivo)

"I'm sexually active!"
That's what she said.
What does that even mean?
Is it another way of saying...?
..."I like to FUCK"!
Although it doesn't necessarily mean...
..."I want to FUCK you".
...Me...
...in this case!
I think she was just making a statement...
...putting it on the "record".
...nothing personal.
...just a matter of fact.
...it tells you where she stands.
That's all.
Nothing more...
...nothing less.
Don't make too much out of it!
Nevertheless...
...l liked it.
I think I'll put it on a t-shirt...
..."Sexually Active".

"The Don"
17.10 2023

Viseral

(Viscerale)

It's a viseral thing...
...that's ALL it is!
Sexual attraction is a *"gut"* feeling.
It happens instantly.
And...
...there's NOTHING you can do about it!
It's out of your control.
It either happens.
Or...
...it doesn't happen.

You cannot *manufacture it.*
You cannot *falsify it.*
You cannot *fake it.*
You cannot *force it.*
You just have to ACCEPT it!
There is no logic to it.
So...
...don't try to analyze it.
...don't try to find a formula.
...don't "overthink" it.
Because...
...it's a viseral thing!

"The Don"
19.10.2023

Books written by "The Don"

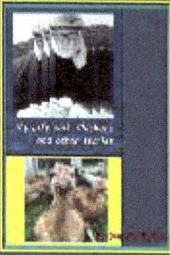

"My Life with Chickens & other stories: I Pity the Poor Immigrant"
Published:
10th September, 2019
Autobiography Book 1:
0 – 12 years old

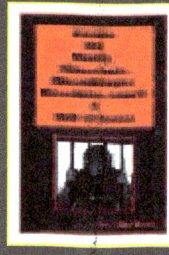

"Poems for Misfits, Miscreants, Misanthropes, Mavericks, Losers & Malcontents!"
Published:
10th June, 2020
Book of Poems 1

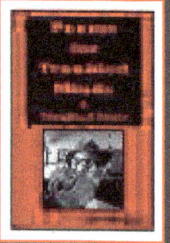

"Poems for Troubled Minds & Trouble Hearts"
Published:
10th August, 2020

Book of Poems 2

"My Life in a CULT & other stories: Everybody Must Get STONED!"
Published:
10th September, 2020
Autobiography Book 2:
15 – 30 years old

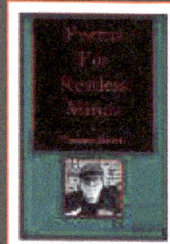

"Poems for Restless Minds & Restless Hearts"
Published:
10th October, 2020
Book of Poems 3

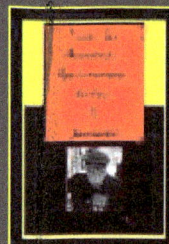

"Poems for Anarchists, Revolutionaries, Outlaws & Dissidents!"
Published:
10th November, 2020

Book of Poems 4

"Poems for Non-Thinkers & Eccentrics"
Published:
10th December, 2020
Book of Poems 5

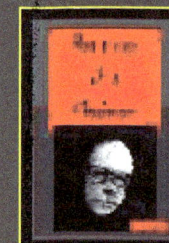

"The Rantings of a Madman"
Published:
10th January, 2021

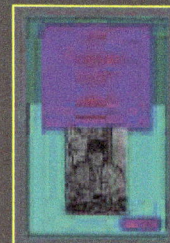

Book of Poems 6

"Poems for Desperate Lovers & Silent Voices"
Published:
10th February, 2021
Book of Poems 7

"Poems for Tormented Minds & Tortured Souls"
Published:
10th March, 2021
Book of Poems 8

All available ONLY online

Books written by "The Don"

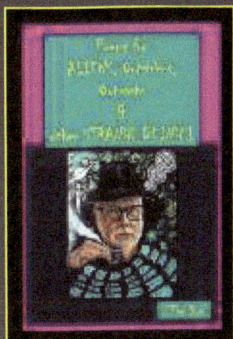

"Poems for ALIENS, Outsiders, Outcasts & other STRANGE BEINGS!"
Published: 10th April, 2021
Book of Poems 9

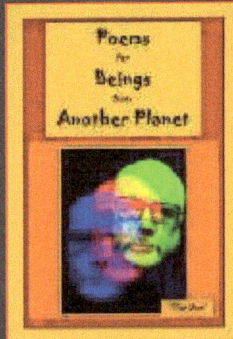

"Poems for Beings From Another Planet"
Published: 10th May, 2021
Book of Poems 10

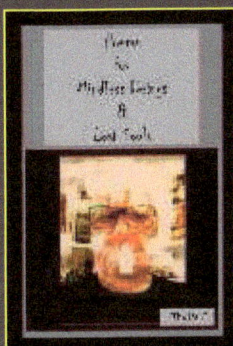

"Poems for Mindless Beings & Lost Souls"
Published: 10th June, 2021
Book of Poems 11

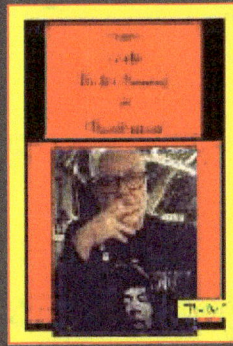

"Poems for the Broken Hearted & Misunderstood
Published: 10th July, 2021
Book of Poems 12

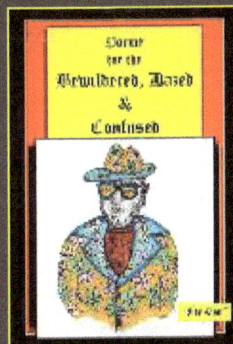

"Poems for Poems for the Bewildered, Dazed & Confused"
10th August, 2021
Book of Poems 13

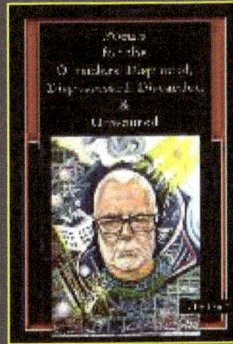

"Poems for the Outsiders, Displaced, Dispossessed, Discarded & Unwanted"
Published: 10th Sept, 2021
Book of Poems 14

All available ONLY online

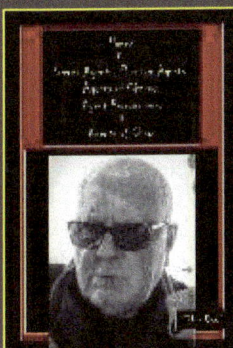

"Poems for Secret Agents, Phantom Agents, Agents of Change, Agent Provocateurs & Agents of Chaos"
Published: 10th Oct, 2021
Book of Poems 15

"Poems for Disenchanted, Disillusioned & Delusional"
Published: 10th November, 2021
Book of Poems 16

Books written by "The Don"

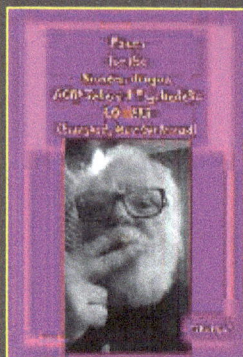

"Poems for the Stoners, drugos, ACID takers & Psychedelic LO❤ERS (Everybody Must Get Stoned)"
Published: 10th December, 2021
Book of Poems 17

"Poems for Anarchists, Rebels & Revolutionaries
Published: 10th January, 2022
Book of Poems 18

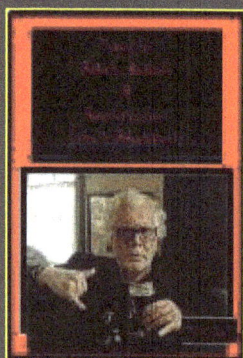

"Poems for Rebels, Radicals & Revolutionaries (Viva la Révolution!)"
Published: 10th February, 2022
Book of Poems 19

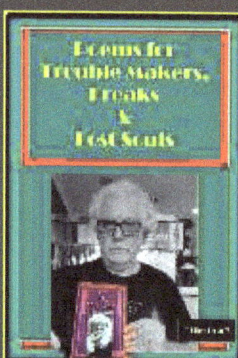

"Poems for Trouble Makers, Freaks & Lost Souls"
Published: 10th March 2022
Book of Poems 20

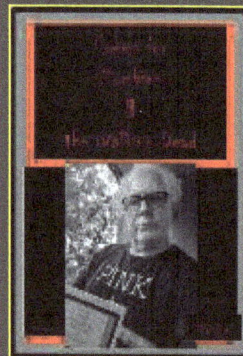

"Poems for Zombies & the Walking Dead"
Published: 10th April 2022
Book of Poems 21

"Poems for Non-Conformists (Never conform!)"
Published: 10th May 2022
Book of Poems 22

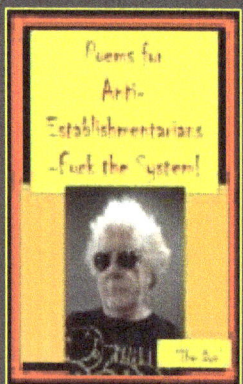

"Poems for Anti-Establishment-arians -Fuck the System!"
Published: 10th June 2022
Book of Poems 23

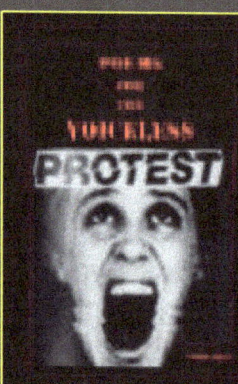

"Poems for the Voiceless"
Published: 10th July 2022
Book of Poems 24

All available ONLY online

Books written by "The Don"

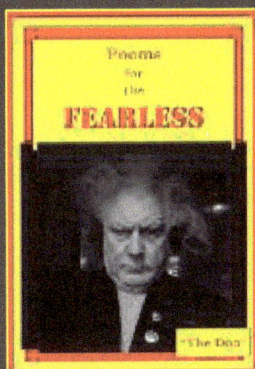

"Poems for the Fearless"

Published: 10th August 2022

Book of Poems 25

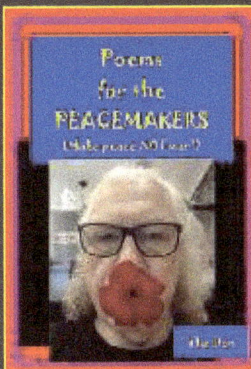

"Poems for the PEACEMAKER: Make peace NOT war!"

Published: 10th March 2023

Book of Poems 26

Poems for the Forever Young (May you stay forever young!)
Published: 10th June 2023
Book of Poems 27

Poems for the Children of the REVOLUTION!
Published: 5th December 2023

Book of Poems 28

All available ONLY online

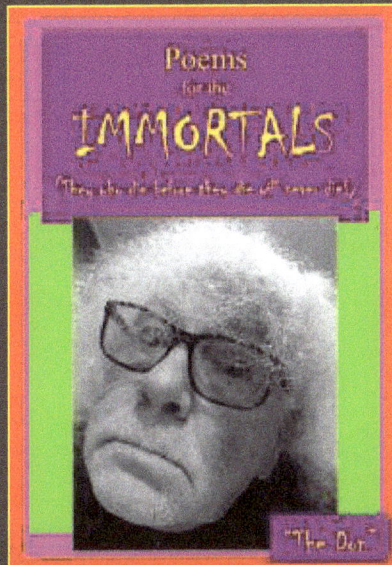

Poems for the L'Innocente!
Published: 10th March 2024
Book of Poems 29

Poems for the IMMORTALS (They who die before they die will never die!)
Published: 10th July 2024
Book of Poems 30

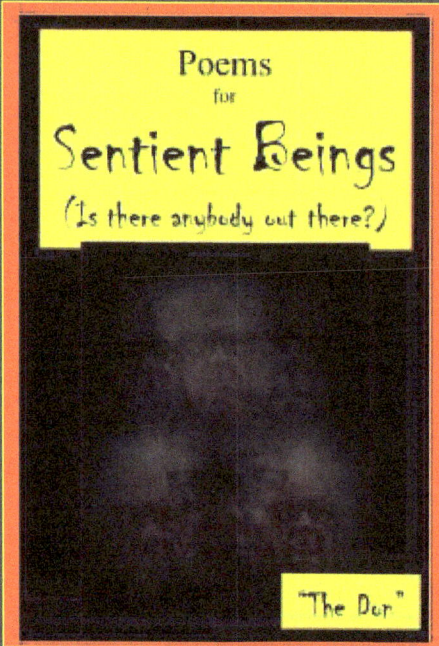

Poems
for
Sentient Beings
(Is there anybody out there?)

"The Don"

Poems for
Sentient Beings
(Is there anybody out
there?)

Published: 10th
December 2024

Book of Poems 31

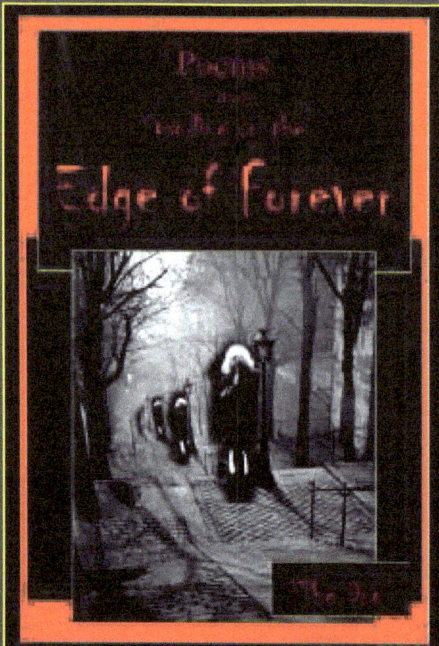

Poems
for
those standing on the
Edge of Forever

Poems for those
Standing on the Edge
of Forever

Published: 10th
December 2024

Book of Poems 32